D1364091

Capybaras

by Rachel Grack

BELLWETHER MEDIA • MINNEAPOLIS, MN

Note to Librarians, Teachers, and Parents:

Blastoff! Readers are carefully developed by literacy experts and combine standards-based content with developmentally appropriate text.

Level 1 provides the most support through repetition of high-frequency words, light text, predictable sentence patterns, and strong visual support.

Level 2 offers early readers a bit more challenge through varied simple sentences, increased text load, and less repetition of high-frequency words.

Level 3 advances early-fluent readers toward fluency through increased text and concept load, less reliance on visuals, longer sentences, and more literary language.

Level 4 builds reading stamina by providing more text per page, increased use of punctuation, greater variation in sentence patterns, and increasingly challenging vocabulary.

Level 5 encourages children to move from "learning to read" to "reading to learn" by providing even more text, varied writing styles, and less familiar topics.

Whichever book is right for your reader, Blastoff! Readers are the perfect books to build confidence and encourage a love of reading that will last a lifetime!

This edition first published in 2019 by Bellwether Media, Inc.

No part of this publication may be reproduced in whole or in part without written permission of the publisher. For information regarding permission, write to Bellwether Media, Inc., Attention: Permissions Department, 6012 Blue Circle Drive, Minnetonka, MN 55343.

Library of Congress Cataloging-in-Publication Data

Names: Koestler-Grack, Rachel A., 1973- author.
Title: Capybaras / by Rachel Grack.
Description: Minneapolis, MN : Bellwether Media, Inc., 2019. |
  Series: Blastoff! Readers. Animals of the Rain forest | Audience: Ages 5-8. |
  Audience: K to grade 3. | Includes bibliographical references and index.
Identifiers: LCCN 2018031002 (print) | LCCN 2018037390 (ebook) |
  ISBN 9781681036724 (ebook) | ISBN 9781626179486 (hardcover : alk. paper)
Subjects: LCSH: Capybara--Juvenile literature. | Rain forest animals--Juvenile literature.
Classification: LCC QL737.R662 (ebook) | LCC QL737.R662 K64 2019 (print) | DDC 599.35/9--dc23
LC record available at https://lccn.loc.gov/2018031002

Editor: Betsy Rathburn   Designer: Jeffrey Kollock

Printed in the United States of America, North Mankato, MN

Table of Contents

Capybaras are the world's largest **rodents**.

They live near water in Central and South America.

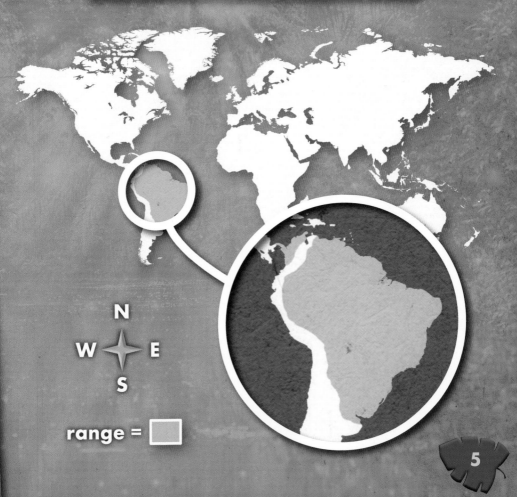

Capybara Range

N
W E
S

range = ☐

These shaggy animals
live in the rain forest.
They love the hot, **humid**
weather of this **biome**!

Their brown fur helps them blend
into muddy rivers, lakes, and ponds.

Capybaras are **adapted** for water. Eyes and **nostrils** on top of their heads help them stay **alert** while swimming.

nostril

Special Adaptations

brown fur

eyes and nostrils
on top of head

webbed feet

Webbed feet help
these rodents swim fast!

Water Wallowers

Capybaras have **scent glands** for marking **territory**. They mark trees and bushes to circle their spaces.

They sometimes mark their favorite **watering holes**!

Capybara Stats

Least Concern	Near Threatened	Vulnerable	Endangered	Critically Endangered	Extinct in the Wild	Extinct

conservation status: least concern

life span: up to 10 years

capybaras in a
watering hole

wallowing

Capybaras like to **wallow** in water and mud. This keeps them cool in the rain forest heat.

Sometimes, **predators** attack! Capybaras dive underwater to escape.

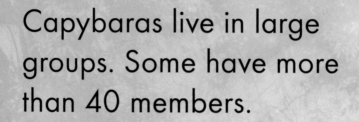

Capybaras live in large groups. Some have more than 40 members.

Some members act as guards.
They bark when danger is near!

When predators are close, young capybaras crowd together in the middle of the group.

The adults form a circle around them to keep them safe.

Chewing Grass

Each day, capybaras chew up to
8 pounds (3.6 kilograms) of grass.

This can be hard to **digest**. Capybaras eat poop to help break down food!

Capybara Diet

water hyacinths

smooth flatsedge

reeds

19

Chewing grass wears down
capybara teeth. But their teeth
never stop growing!

Capybaras **thrive** in their rain forest **habitat**!

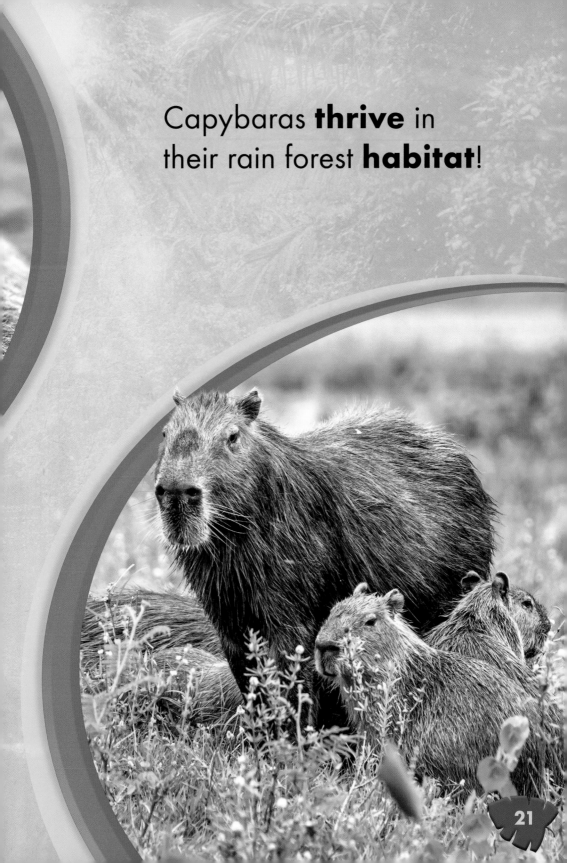

Glossary

adapted—well suited due to changes over a long period of time

alert—quick to notice or act

biome—a large area with certain plants, animals, and weather

digest—to break down food

habitat—the place where an animal lives

humid—hot and wet

nostrils—the two openings of the nose

predators—animals that hunt other animals for food

rodents—animals that gnaw on their food

scent glands—body parts that spray odor

territory—the land area where an animal lives

thrive—to grow well

wallow—to roll in mud or water

watering holes—pools of water from which animals drink

To Learn More

AT THE LIBRARY

Hansen, Grace. *Capybaras*. Minneapolis, Minn.: Abdo Kids, 2017.

Morey, Allan. *Capybaras*. Mankato, Minn.: Amicus Ink, 2018.

Statts, Leo. *Capybaras*. Minneapolis, Minn.: Abdo Zoom, 2017.

ON THE WEB

FACTSURFER

Factsurfer.com gives you a safe, fun way to find more information.

1. Go to www.factsurfer.com.

2. Enter "capybaras" into the search box.

3. Click the "Surf" button and select your book cover to see a list of related web sites.

Index

The images in this book are reproduced through the courtesy of: Vladislav T. Jirousek, front cover, p. 1; RicardoKuhl, pp. 4-5; Hans Wagemaker, p. 6; elleon, pp. 6-7; Maarten Zeehandelaar, pp. 8-9; Musat, p. 9; SutidaS, p. 9 (inset); buteo, pp. 10, 23; Vadim Petrakov, pp. 10-11, 12-13, 21; Uwe Bergwitz, p. 13; Massis, p. 14; William Mullins/ Alamy, pp. 14-15; Bruno Vieira, p. 16; SeppFriedhuber, pp. 16-17; Alexandr Vorobev, pp. 18-19; Steve Cymro, p. 19 (top left); Forest & Kim Starr/ Wikipedia, p. 19 (top right); bejdova, p. 19 (bottom); kyslynskahal, pp. 20-21.